P9-BHX-398

DISASTER ALERT!

TRANSPORTATION DISASTER ALERT!

Niki Walker

Crabtree Publishing Company
www.crabtreebooks.com

presented by:

Crabtree Publishing Company
www.crabtreebooks.com

Coordinating editor: Ellen Rodger

Editor: Carrie Gleason

Copyediting: Rachel Eagen, Adrianna Morganelli

Book design and production coordinator: Rosie Gowsell

Layout and production assistance: Samara Parent

Scanning technician: Arlene Arch-Wilson

Art director: Rob MacGregor

Photo research: Allison Napier

Photographs: AP Wide World Photos: p. 14, p. 15, p.16 (bottom); Bettmann/Corbis: cover; p. 5 (bottom), pp. 8-9, p. 10, p. 11 (bottom), p. 24, p. 26, p. 27; David Butow/Corbis SABA: p. 20; Mark Cooper/Corbis: p. 12 (top); Steve Crise/Corbis: p. 4; Patrick Durand/Corbis Sygma: p. 9 (bottom); Najlah Feanny/Corbis SABA: p. 3; Stephen Frink/zefa/Corbis: p. 1; Nicolas Gouhier/Corbis/Sygma: p. 22 (bottom); Ralf-Finn Hestoft/Corbis: p. 6; Hulton-Deutsch Collection/Corbis: p. 5 (top); David Loh/Reuters/Corbis: p. 21; Reuters/Corbis: p. 13, p. 23, p. 29; Alan Schein/zefa/Corbis: p. 16 (top); Stringer/USA/Reuters/Corbis: p. 7; Transportation Safety Board of Canada/Reuters/Corbis: p. 31; Tim Wright/Corbis: p. 30; Yogi, Inc./Corbis: p. 12 (bottom); Jay Directo/Getty Images: p. 28; Christophe Simaon/Getty Images: p. 17. Other images from stock photo cd

Illustrations: Dan Pressman: p. 18-19

Cover: When trains derail, they come off their tracks. This train derailed after it hit another train parked on the track.

Contents: Airplanes not only crash in the air, some also crash even before they leave the runway. This plane floated down a runway after the airport was severely flooded.

Title page: Some shipwrecks can be recovered and brought back up to the surface. Others are left at the bottom of the sea.

Crabtree Publishing Company
www.crabtreebooks.com   1-800-387-7650

Cataloging-in-Publication Data
Walker, Niki, 1972-
  Transportation disaster alert! / written by Niki Walker.
    p. cm. -- (Disaster alert!)
  Includes index.
  ISBN-13: 978-0-7787-1584-9 (rlb)
  ISBN-10: 0-7787-1584-1 (rlb)
  ISBN-13: 978-0-7787-1616-7 (pbk)
  ISBN-10: 0-7787-1616-3 (pbk)
  1. Transportation accidents--Juvenile literature. 2. Transportation accidents--Juvenile literature--Pictorial works. 3. Traffic safety--Juvenile literature. I. Title. II. Series.
  HE194.W35 2005
  363.12'063--dc22
                  2005019030
                        LC

Published in the United States
PMB 16A
350 Fifth Ave.,
Suite 3308
New York, NY
10118

Published in Canada
616 Welland Ave.,
St. Catharines,
Ontario, Canada
L2M 5V6

Published in the United Kingdom
73 Lime Walk,
Headington,
Oxford
OX3 7AD
United Kingdom

Published in Australia
386 Mt. Alexander Rd.,
Ascot Vale (Melbourne)
VIC 3032

Table of Contents

Accidents Happen

Every day, ships, trucks, airplanes, and trains move people and goods across land and oceans. Most trips end without any problems but sometimes accidents happen. These accidents become transportation disasters when they result in the injury or death of many people or damage the environment.

Better transportation

People are continually searching for ways to travel faster, farther, and more safely. Centuries ago, the only way to cross the Atlantic Ocean was in wooden ships, which stood a good chance of shipwreck. Today, people fly safely and comfortably from North America to Europe in just a few hours. New technology, such as **radar**, **GPS**, and **satellites**, has made transportation safer than ever. Yet accidents still happen and quickly turn into disasters as ships, trains, and planes have become bigger, travel faster, and hold more passengers than ever before.

What is a disaster?
A disaster is a destructive event that affects the natural world and human communities. Some disasters are predictable, but others occur without warning. Coping successfully with a disaster depends on a community's preparation.

3134   3134

WESTRAIL

Transportation disasters, such as this train wreck, are made much worse when the vehicle's cargo includes flammable or explosive material.

When mechanical parts of vehicles fail, transportation accidents can happen. The brakes on this plane stopped working, causing the plane to crash into a railway line. No one on board was killed, thanks to the quick thinking of a specially trained pilot.

Essex, England, 1960

The Bermuda Triangle

For centuries, strange tales have been told about an area of the Atlantic Ocean known as the Bermuda Triangle. More than 150 plane and ship disappearances have been recorded in the area. Often, the ships and planes have vanished without a trace within short distances of land. Some people believe the disappearances were caused by sudden storms, compass failures, tornados at sea called waterspouts, or the mistakes of pilots or sailors. Others believe the Bermuda Triangle is a great unsolved mystery.

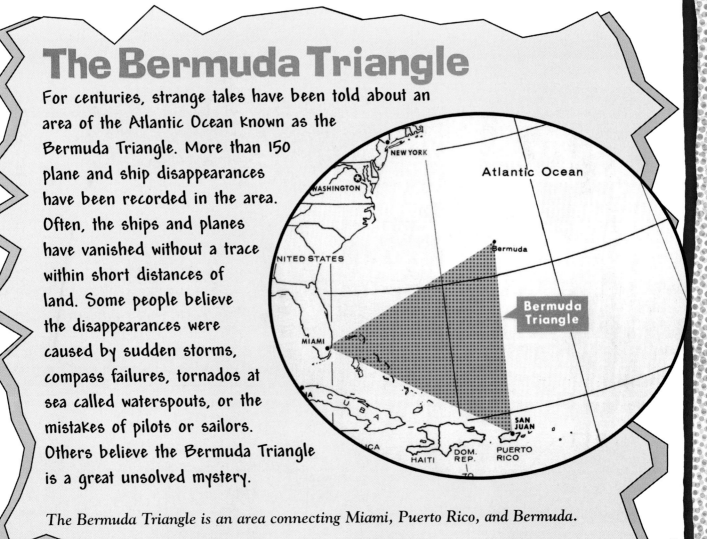

The Bermuda Triangle is an area connecting Miami, Puerto Rico, and Bermuda.

Disaster in the Making

Safe transportation relies on trained people working with well-made and maintained equipment. Disasters can happen when part of a vehicle breaks, electronic equipment stops working, or people make mistakes.

Human error

Human error, or a person making a mistake, is the most common cause of transportation disasters. Every day, thousands of people are involved in getting planes, ships, and trains safely from one place to another. Many of these people work behind the scenes. Mechanics thoroughly and carefully inspect, maintain, and repair vehicles to keep them running safely. People who control the flow of traffic in harbors, on railways, and in airports keep track of many vehicles at once and guide them safely around one another to avoid collisions. Pilots, ship captains, and rail engineers must be alert, in control of their vehicle, and able to make good decisions quickly. Disasters happen when any one of these people are careless, make a bad decision, or ignore a dangerous situation.

Jobs that seem small, such as changing lightbulbs, can help save people's lives. Maintenance crew have as little time as 25 minutes between flights to ensure an airplane is ready for the next takeoff.

6

Equipment failure

Today's planes, trains, and ships are complex machines with thousands of parts. Even the bolts that hold them together are specially made to withstand **pressure** and weather. Sophisticated engines and computerized **navigation** equipment make them run and help them find their way. Equipment failure happens when any one of these parts stops working properly. Equipment can fail because it is poorly designed or made, it has not been properly maintained, or it is worn out. Structural failure happens when part of a vehicle breaks apart or falls off because it is too weak or too worn.

Weather watch

Strong winds can blow vehicles off course and make them difficult to steer. Blizzards, fog, and heavy rains can make it almost impossible to see the way ahead, which can lead to a collision. Weather puts strain on pilots, train engineers, and ship captains, as well as stress on the vehicles. Severe storms can whip up high, powerful waves that break apart ships, and heavy winds and **turbulence** can shake planes hard enough to cause structural damage. Very strong winds can even blow trains right off their tracks!

Severe weather can lead to equipment failure and human error. Disasters are often caused by a combination of these factors.

On The Sea

Every day, massive ships cross the oceans with their cargoes and boats ferry thousands of passengers across channels and oceans. Ships today are made of sturdy steel and carry the latest technology for navigation, weather reports, and safety. Even with this new technology, the ocean can be a dangerous and unforgiving place.

Mistakes at sea

Human error is the cause of most shipping disasters. In some cases, ships collide with other ships, icebergs, or rocks. Most collisions occur because the captain or crew do not follow proper **procedure**, they misinterpret the situation, or they cannot see through the fog. In other cases, ships capsize, or tip over, because their cargo is improperly loaded and has shifted. Ships also sink under the weight of their cargo if they are overloaded. In some cases, poor design or poor construction has caused ships to leak or break apart at sea.

The greatest sea rescue happened in 1956, when the Andrea Doria sank off the coast of Massachusetts. The Andrea Doria was struck by another boat, the Stockholm, in heavy fog. The damage was so severe that the crew could not use the ship's lifeboats. Rescue ships arrived in time to save 1,663 of the 1,706 people aboard the ship.

(below)
People check dead and missing lists after a ferry disaster in the Philippines. On December 20, 1987, the Dona Paz passenger ship sank after an inexperienced sailor crashed it into an oil tanker and it caught fire. Only 24 of about 4,000 passengers survived.

Why boats float

Passenger and cargo ships are massive steel or iron objects that float on water. Ships float because of a **force** called **buoyancy**. An object on water that is buoyant has an equal amount of force pushing it down on the water as the force pushing it up. Buoyancy depends on **density** and **displacement**. To be buoyant, a ship has to be less dense than the water. Ships are specially designed so that their weight is spread out over a very large area. Most of what is inside a ship is air, which is less dense than water. A ship's large, curved shape also displaces, or moves aside, a lot of water. As long as a ship weighs less than the amount of water it displaces, it will float.

Why boats sink

Ships sink when they take on water, usually through a hole in the hull, or outer shell. Water rushes into a ship, replacing the air. Water is more dense than air, so the ship's density increases until the boat weighs more than the water it displaces, and sinks.

Rough seas

Rough weather at sea puts great stress on the crew and the ship. As a ship gets tossed up and down and lashed by one powerful wave after another, the crew has to try to keep the ship pointed head-on into the waves. If the ship broaches, or turns sideways to the waves, it may be pushed over.

Ships that broach can take on water and capsize. Sometimes rough seas are simply too much for a boat to withstand, no matter how well the crew reacts. A ship may spring a leak and sink, or it may break apart because of the force of the waves.

The Halifax Explosion

On December 6, 1917, the collision of two ships in Halifax Harbor, Nova Scotia, Canada, triggered the second-biggest explosion in history. Many war ships were in the harbor that day, preparing to head overseas to fight in World War I. Two ships, the *Mont-Blanc* and the *Imo*, tried to navigate past one another through a narrow stretch in the harbor, but the *Imo* struck the *Mont-Blanc*. A fire broke out on the *Mont-Blanc*, which was loaded with dynamite and other explosives. The crew abandoned ship and rowed for shore in lifeboats. A short time later, the *Mont-Blanc* exploded, blowing apart buildings and sparking fires in the city of Halifax.

More than 1,900 people in Halifax were killed, and 4,000 were injured in the explosion.

The survival factors

When ships begin to sink, many factors determine whether or not the people onboard survive. Ships may sink in minutes or hours, depending on their damage, and that difference affects whether passengers have enough warning time to reach lifeboats. If a ship goes down in cold or rough waters, people will not survive long in the water. If other boats or rescue vehicles are close by and arrive quickly, many people can be pulled from the water alive. In the past, many disasters were made worse because the captain and crew did not take charge. They either abandoned passengers to save themselves, or they did not lead people through emergency drills at the start of the voyage.

A life preserver is thrown to a person in the water to keep them afloat until they are rescued.

Hakodate, Japan, 1954

In 1954, the fierce winds of a typhoon capsized the Toya Maru *ferry off Japan, killing more than 1,100 people. In this photo, people scan coffins for missing relatives who did not survive.*

Beneath the Sea

Submarines are large, sturdy ships that can submerge, or go completely under water. Subs are used by militaries to patrol oceans, spy on other countries, and carry missiles. Submarines can be deadly places for their crews when something goes wrong.

How subs work

Submarines are specially designed to take in water, which allows them to submerge. They have a hollow area between an inner and outer hull that can be filled with water or emptied. This hollow area is called the ballast tank. To make the sub dive, or sink, the crew opens holes in the outer hull and the ballast tank fills with water. To raise the sub, the crew releases air from a separate tank into the ballast tank, which forces out the water. As the ballast tank fills with air, the sub begins to rise.

There is a limited amount of air in a submarine. If a sub breaks down under water, the crew must be rescued before their air supply runs out. The Sea Cliff is a Deep Submergence Vehicle that can dive 20,000 feet (6,096 meters) to rescue a sub's crew.

Under pressure

Water pressure is the force that water exerts on submerged objects. Water pressure increases with depth, so the deeper that subs travel beneath the surface, the greater the amount of force pressing in on them. Subs are built to withstand this force. Any weakness in a sub's hull causes it to crumple.

Disasters in the deep

When subs submerge, every opening, including **air vents**, valves, and hatches, or doors, must be sealed perfectly. Even the smallest leaks lead to disaster, as water damages electronic equipment and shuts down the sub's power supply. Without power, a sub has no way to reach the surface. Leaks also destroy subs by filling them with extra water so quickly that the subs sink to the bottom under the weight.

Life support

The deep ocean is cold and dark and the water pressure is immense. It is not a place where people can survive on their own, so subs are equipped with life-support systems. A life-support system is made up of equipment that provides the crew with air to breathe, fresh water to drink, and a comfortable temperature in which to live. The equipment is powered by the sub's **nuclear reactor** or **diesel engines**. When subs sink and power goes out, batteries take over to power the system.

Submarine crews are equipped with escape suits, which can help them survive when a sub sinks in shallow water. The suit floats and keeps sailors warm, protects them from fire, and allows them to breathe.

Explosions

Most subs are armed with torpedoes, missiles, or other explosives. If these weapons accidentally explode, part of the sub, or the whole sub, can be destroyed. Many subs today are powered by nuclear reactors. These reactors must be kept cool in order to work safely. When reactors overheat, **radiation** can escape. Radiation makes people extremely ill and in large amounts it can kill. If a reactor overheats too much, it can lead to a meltdown, or the destruction of the reactor. A meltdown ends in an explosion that spreads radiation into the water around the sub and the air above it.

When the U.S.S. Squalus sank on a test dive off the coast of New Hampshire, a diving bell was sent to rescue the crew. Here, workmen in the rescue diving bell try to get to the scene in time to save the trapped crew. In the end, 33 of the 59 crew aboard the Squalus were rescued through the diving bell.

The U.S.S. Squalus *was returned to the surface after it sunk.*

The First Rescue

Until the 1930s, rescue equipment for sailors trapped aboard sunken submarines did not exist. After a series of sub accidents in the 1920s, Charles Momsen invented an **escape capsule** that was lowered to a sub and attached with a watertight seal. Sailors were saved by climbing into the capsule, which was hauled up to the surface. The capsule was first used in 1939, to save 33 men who were trapped 243 feet (74 meters) below the ocean's surface in the U.S.S. *Squalus*. The U.S.S. *Squalus* sank because one of its air valves was open even though the sub's control board showed it to be sealed. When the sub dove, water flooded the engine room. The weight of the water quickly dragged the sub down to the ocean floor.

On the Rails

Trains became a popular method of transportation in the 1800s. They have gone through many changes and improvements since then, and today trains are one of the safest methods of transportation in the world. Still, rail workers occasionally make mistakes, equipment sometimes fails, and disasters such as collisions and derailments result.

Solon Springs, Wisconsin, 2005

In training

Rail conductors and engineers are highly skilled. Conductors train for up to two years at college, using **simulators** and real railroad equipment to practice working under regular and emergency conditions. After a few years on the job, conductors can become engineers by completing more specialized training and then passing tests that demonstrate their ability to control trains and make wise decisions under pressure.

Derailments

A train can derail, or come off the track, when an engineer takes it around a curve too quickly or tries to stop too quickly. Cracks or breaks in a rail or flawed wheels can also cause derailments. Strong winds can also blow trains off their tracks.

(above) People living close to this train wreck were evacuated from their homes until it was found no harmful chemicals were on board.

Collisions

Train collisions involve human error. In some cases, one engineer does not realize that another train has stopped on the tracks ahead. In other cases, two trains hurtle toward one another on the same track. Usually, these collisions are the result of signal errors. Signals are used to communicate to engineers. Signals tell engineers to slow down, proceed, or stop. In the past, signals were signs posted by signal workers who kept track of the trains passing through their section of railway. Many collisions were caused because signal workers made mistakes, but engineers also made errors. Sometimes engineers misunderstood a signal, other times they simply ignored it. Today, rail signals are colored lights, and each color has a different meaning. Most signals are run by computers. They are maintained by highly trained workers.

In many parts of the world, trains are the main method of transportation, and they carry thousands of passengers at a time. Other trains carry goods. In this rail accident in Spain, a passenger train and a cargo train collided. The accident was caused by human error when the passenger train was given the go-ahead to proceed before the cargo train had passed. Many people were injured in the accident and some were killed.

Chinchilla, Spain, 2003

In the Air

Each year, there are millions of military and commercial airplane and jet flights, and crashes are extremely rare. Aircrafts travel at such great speeds and heights that when something goes wrong, the potential for disaster is huge.

The physics of flight

There are four main forces at work on all planes—from small **propeller**-driven airplanes to large passenger jets—as they get off the ground and fly through the air. These forces are lift, thrust, gravity, and drag. The forces must be kept in balance to keep the plane in the air and under control.

> The rudder changes the plane's direction.

> Drag works against thrust, tugging backward against the plane as it moves through the air.

> Elevators on the tail control the plane's pitch—whether its nose points up, down, or straight ahead.

Control

Crashes happen for a variety of reasons, many of which are beyond the pilot's control. Crashes may occur when one or more of a plane's engines shut down due to mechanical problems. Without enough power, it is difficult to generate enough thrust to keep a plane in the air. Crashes are also caused when one of the control surfaces stops working. Airplane control surfaces are the elevator, rudder, and ailerons, which allow the pilot to control and steer the plane.

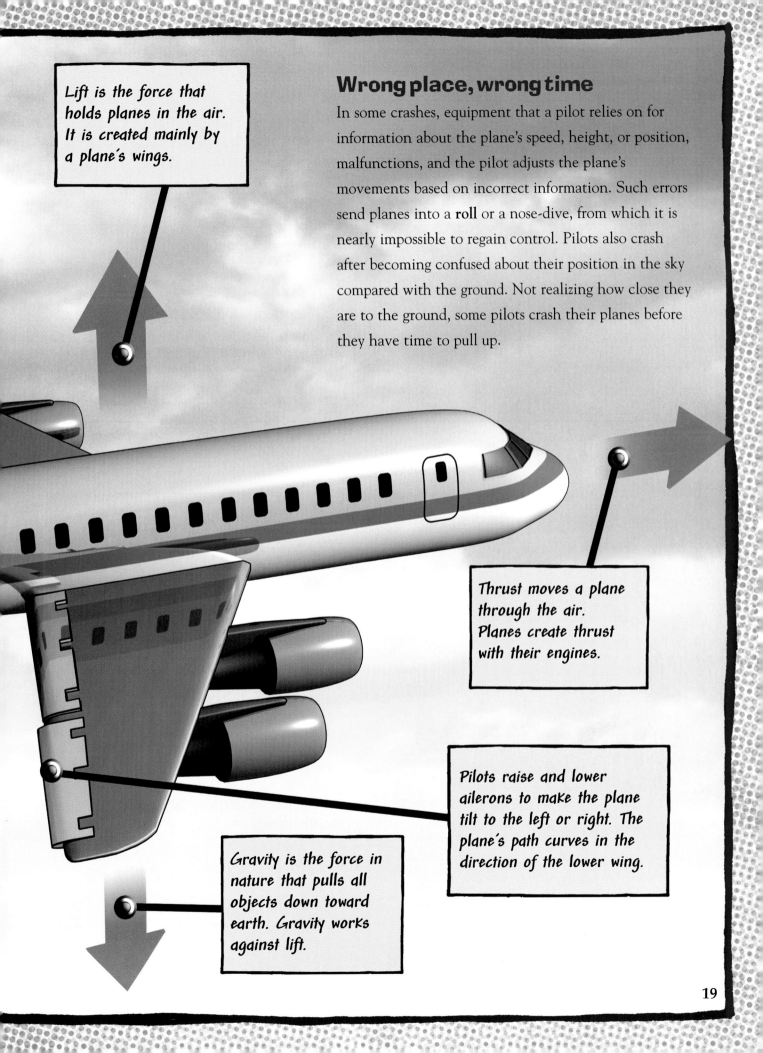

Lift is the force that holds planes in the air. It is created mainly by a plane's wings.

Wrong place, wrong time

In some crashes, equipment that a pilot relies on for information about the plane's speed, height, or position, malfunctions, and the pilot adjusts the plane's movements based on incorrect information. Such errors send planes into a **roll** or a nose-dive, from which it is nearly impossible to regain control. Pilots also crash after becoming confused about their position in the sky compared with the ground. Not realizing how close they are to the ground, some pilots crash their planes before they have time to pull up.

Thrust moves a plane through the air. Planes create thrust with their engines.

Pilots raise and lower ailerons to make the plane tilt to the left or right. The plane's path curves in the direction of the lower wing.

Gravity is the force in nature that pulls all objects down toward earth. Gravity works against lift.

Air traffic controllers

At airports, planes take off and land on the same runways. Air traffic controllers keep track of which planes are **taxiing**, taking off, and landing at all times to avoid collisions. They assign planes runways and make sure the planes do not cross paths. Other controllers guide planes in for safe landings. Some flights end in disaster before the planes even leave the ground because of mistakes made by pilots or air traffic controllers. Fires often follow ground collisions when the fuel on one or both planes bursts into flames. In the air, planes are monitored by people on the ground to make sure the planes in their airspace are a safe distance apart. They track the planes with radar and speak with the pilots using radios. Air traffic controllers instruct pilots to fly higher or lower to avoid other planes or rough weather.

Experts believe that about 80 percent of air crashes are caused by human error. In the past, these accidents were blamed on "pilot error," but this term is misleading. Many people are involved in a flight, including mechanics, ground crews, air traffic controllers, and flight crew. Any of them can make a mistake that leads to a plane crash.

Commercial pilots

It takes hundreds of hours of flying time, as well as years of training and working on the job, to become a certified commercial pilot. Commercial pilots must have their instrument rating, which allows them to fly in conditions with poor **visibility**. Pilots encounter a variety of conditions in the air, all of which affect how a plane moves. Pilots train to deal with storms and winds as well as **thermals**, **mountain waves**, **wind shears**, and other forms of turbulence, or air disturbances. These disturbances can cause a plane to suddenly rise, drop, or shake and shudder. To earn their instrument rating, pilots must pass a classroom course, **log** a certain number of hours flying in poor visibility, and pass a flying test. Pilots also need a multi-engine rating, which allows them to fly planes with more than one engine. These are the planes used by most airlines.

Simulators

Pilots train in real planes, but they also spend many hours training on flight simulators. Simulators are working models of cockpits, or the area where the pilot and copilot sit, that allow pilots to practice reacting to unusual and emergency situations, such as engine failure, which is too dangerous to practice in the air. Simulators have **instrument panels** that imitate those of planes in flight, allowing pilots to see and feel the effects of their maneuvers and decisions as if they were actually flying. Pilots gain experience and quickly learn what to do and what not to do in various emergency situations.

(above) Flight simulators are operated by computers. The screen in front of the pilot shows what a real life situation looks like.

On the Highways

Cars and trucks are the most common forms of transportation in North America. Accidents become disasters when many vehicles are involved in a single chain reaction crash known as a pileup.

What are pileups?

Pileups usually start as accidents involving one or two vehicles. Cars and trucks behind those in the accident cannot stop or swerve in time to avoid the collision, and one vehicle after another slams into the car ahead of it. Pileups can happen on city streets, but they are most common on highways, where vehicles travel at high speeds.

One law of physics states that a body in motion tends to stay in motion. Motion is movement. Passengers in moving cars and trucks are bodies in motion, so when their vehicles suddenly stop, their bodies naturally keep moving. They do not stop until something forces them to. Seat belts help save lives because they force passengers to stop moving when their vehicles do.

Momentum

Cars and trucks moving at high speeds do not stop the instant drivers hit their brakes because they have a lot of momentum. Momentum is the **energy** of an object in motion. It is the result of an object's velocity, or speed, and **mass**. Cars and trucks on highways have a lot of momentum because they have a lot of mass, or are large and heavy, and they are moving fast. Pileups are especially disastrous because when vehicles slam into each other, they are forced to a sudden stop, and the energy of their momentum is transferred to the other vehicles they hit.

Disastrous results

Pileups happen so quickly that drivers usually do not have time to get out of their cars before other vehicles slam into them. Vehicles can be sandwiched between one another, which makes it difficult for emergency crews to free the people trapped inside. When pileups involve transport trucks hauling explosive or **flammable** materials, the crash can trigger a fire that quickly spreads to other vehicles. Cargoes of dangerous chemicals or gases can also be released by a crash. The chemicals and gases may damage the environment and make people sick.

Drivers on highways do not always leave enough space between their vehicles and those ahead of them. When vehicles in front suddenly brake, drivers cannot stop in time to avoid hitting them.

23

Famous Disasters

All transportation disasters are unexpected and very sad events, especially for the families of people involved. Some disasters are so shocking that they stun the entire world.

The *Titanic*

When the *Titanic* left England on April 10, 1912, its passengers were thrilled to be part of the luxury ship's first voyage across the Atlantic. The *Titanic* was advertised as "unsinkable." No one suspected that they would soon be part of the world's worst shipping disaster. *Titanic* was built using the latest technology and had 16 watertight compartments that could be sealed to keep the ship from flooding if the hull was punctured.

> Ships built since the Titanic have double hulls, which are made up of two layers of steel with about five feet (1.5 meters) of space between them. If the outer layer of steel is punctured, water pours into the space between the layers and does not enter the ship.

North Atlantic Ocean, 1912

The unthinkable happens

At first, all went well as the *Titanic* steamed across the ocean in record time. As the *Titanic* entered the waters around Newfoundland, the crew began receiving reports of icebergs in the area. Instead of slowing down, the captain kept the ship steaming ahead. At 11:35 p.m. on April 14, one of the crew spotted an iceberg in the *Titanic*'s path, but it was too late. The ship scraped against it less than a minute later, and water began pouring into the *Titanic*. At first, passengers did not realize the seriousness of the situation, and many left in lifeboats that were less than half full. People began to panic when the ship's bow dipped under water and it became clear that there were not enough lifeboats for everyone. By 2:20 a.m., the *Titanic* had disappeared below the waves, and more than 1,500 people died in the freezing water.

Ice Patrol

After the *Titanic* sank, many countries worked together to form the International Ice Patrol to monitor for icebergs. Today, the Ice Patrol uses satellites, ships, and planes to track the movement of icebergs. The *Titanic* disaster also led to other safety rules:

* Ocean liners must carry enough lifeboats to hold every passenger onboard.
* The crew must lead passengers in an emergency drill at the start of the trip.
* Ships must staff their radio rooms 24 hours a day.

The *Hindenburg*

During the 1920s and 1930s, dirigibles, or airships, were a luxurious way for wealthy people to travel. Dirigibles were similar to blimps, but they had a rigid metal frame. The frame was surrounded by a number of bags filled with a gas called hydrogen, which lifted the dirigible into the air. The world's largest dirigible, the *Hindenburg*, was 804 feet (245 meters) long and reached speeds up to 85 miles per hour (137 km/h). On the evening of May 6, 1937, the *Hindenburg* was preparing to land in New Jersey after a trip across the Atlantic Ocean from Germany. Just as the ship approached the landing strip, it burst into flames. In just 32 seconds, the *Hindenburg* was completely burned.

Some people jumped from the ship and survived, but 15 passengers and 20 crew were killed in the fire. The days of airships were over. People are still not sure what caused the *Hindenburg* disaster. Some believe a spark of **static electricity** caused the hydrogen aboard the ship to explode. Others believe it was a spark from the engine.

The Hindenburg's fabric shell was coated in a material like that used to fuel rocket boosters today. Some people believe the fabric, and not the hydrogen inside, caused the Hindenburg disaster.

Lakehurst, New Jersey, 1937

Unlike most disasters, the sinking of the *Lusitania* was not an accident. During World War I, Germany warned England that waters around the island were a war zone. On May 1, 1915, 1,906 passengers set sail from New York aboard the *Lusitania* bound for England. A German sub fired a single torpedo which tore apart the passenger ship. In total, 1,198 people died in the *Lusitania* disaster. Bodies of victims were plucked from the water and buried in a common grave.

The *Kursk*

The *Kursk* submarine was the pride of Russia's navy. It was designed to withstand a direct hit from a torpedo, and Russia described it as "indestructible." On August 12, 2002, the *Kursk* submerged in the Barents Sea, in the Arctic Ocean, for practice exercises. As sailors were preparing to practice a torpedo attack, an explosion suddenly ripped through the torpedo room. Two minutes later, a massive explosion destroyed most of the sub. Of the 118 men onboard, 23 survived the blasts and sealed themselves into a compartment, hoping to be rescued. At the surface, navy leaders watching the practice were shocked.

They did not believe the *Kursk* had sunk and waited several hours before issuing an alert for help. More than 30 hours after the explosion, a Russian rescue vehicle arrived at the scene. Divers tried for days to **dock** the vehicle on the sub but could not get close enough. At first, the Russian government refused offers of help from other countries. The *Kursk* had been carrying top-secret new missiles that the government wanted to keep quiet. After a week, the Russian government accepted help from Norwegian divers. When the divers reached the sub and opened the hatch, they found the *Kursk* flooded and all 23 trapped sailors dead.

S.O.S. Rescue

When a plane, train, or ship is in trouble, its crew **usually sends out a** distress call **for help and to give rescuers their location. A distress call sends emergency workers such as police, firefighters, medical workers, or the Coast Guard into action.**

Distress signals

There are just a few signals that people recognize universally to mean a ship or plane is in trouble. One signal, S.O.S., is sent using Morse code. Morse code uses dashes and dots to represent letters of the alphabet. S.O.S. is represented by three dots, three dashes, and three dots (··· − − − ···). Another distress call is the word "Mayday." It is used to signal that a ship or plane is in immediate danger of sinking or crashing. People call, "Mayday! Mayday! Mayday!" and then give their vehicle's name and location. Most ships and planes also have **emergency beacons** onboard. These beacons are designed to sense water or a sudden impact, so they automatically send radio or satellite signals when a ship sinks or a plane crashes. They repeatedly send out the signals and give the ship's or plane's location.

At sea, victims of disasters are sometimes rescued by helicopters. A person on a winch is lowered from the helicopter to the person in the water. The victim is then attached to the rescuer and both are pulled up to safety.

Search and rescue

When emergency workers receive a distress signal, their first aim is to find the vehicle in trouble. This stage is called search and rescue. Search and rescue is carried out by the military, police, Coast Guard, or volunteer organizations. In remote areas, planes or helicopters are used to search because they can cover large areas quickly.

(below) Rescue workers climb into a crashed plane to search for survivors.

At the scene

When rescuers arrive at the scene of a disaster, there is a series of steps they follow. Their first goal is to find survivors, free them from the wreckage, and give them medical care. The survivors may be rushed to nearby hospitals in ambulances or helicopters. If there are dangerous materials at the scene that may cause a fire, explosion, or sickness, workers also focus on containing them quickly. At plane crash sites, jet fuel is a major concern because it burns very quickly and very hot—between 800°F and 1,500°F (426°C and 815°C). Commercial jets carry thousands of gallons of fuel.

Lessons Learned

From transportation disasters, people can learn more about how to prevent them from happening in the future. Experts spend a great deal of time studying disasters and their causes.

Determining the cause

Investigators are people who study a disaster and try to determine its cause. They rely on evidence they find at the disaster scene. They study the appearance of the wreckage, where and how it lay, what marks it made on the ground as it crashed, and other details. Investigators also collect information about the vehicle's history as well as the history of the people operating it. Knowing these details can help investigators piece together how the disaster unfolded, which can help them rule out some causes and suggest others. The process can be slow. It often takes several months or even years to determine the cause of a disaster. The cause of some transportation disasters are never fully understood.

Automobile manufacturers test their vehicles to ensure passenger safety. Crash test dummies are placed in the vehicles during the tests. By monitoring the dummies during the crash test, examiners can judge how real people might be saved during collisions.

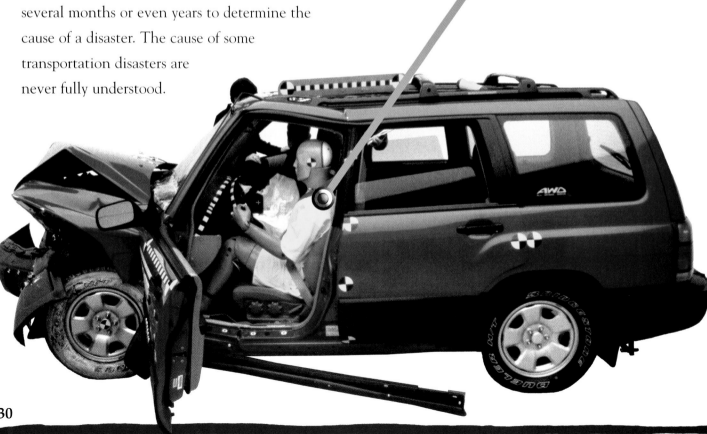

Black boxes

All commercial airplanes and passenger ships carry data recorders, or "black boxes." Data recorders are devices that record information about how the ship was sailing or how the plane was flying. Planes also carry a second recorder called a cockpit voice recorder. It records sounds in the cockpit. This recorder catches everything the pilot and copilot say as well as any noises in the background. Black boxes are designed to withstand disasters, so they provide investigators with a lot of information that help them determine the cause of the accident.

Safer travel

From studying past disasters, people develop new rules, technology, training procedures, and other measures to improve travelers' chances of avoiding and surviving disasters. The list below highlights some of the most important improvements of the past 40 years.

* improved fuel systems for airplanes to reduce fires and explosions
* increased testing of planes to prevent structural failure
* drug and alcohol testing for people who operate trains and planes
* safety devices aboard planes that monitor the distance to the ground and mountains and the distance of other planes. These devices sound alerts when they are too close.
* improved training for crews on planes, ships, and trains to handle unexpected situations
* limiting the number of hours crews can work without sleep
* informing passengers at the start of a trip what to do in case of emergency

Glossary

air vents Parts of a submarine that can be opened or closed to fill the ballast tank with air

buoyancy The upward force that a fluid exerts on less dense objects to keep them afloat

commercial For profit or gain

density The measure of how closely packed the parts of an object are

diesel engine A type of engine that burns oil

displacement The weight of water moved by a ship

distress call A call for help

dock To land on a specific place

emergency beacon Small radio transmitter that gives a ship's position

energy The power, or ability of an object to do work

escape capsule A diving bell that is attached to a sunken submarine's hatch through which trapped crew can enter the bell and return to the surface

flammable Able to catch fire easily

force A push or a pull exerted on an object

GPS Global Positioning System, a worldwide navigational system that uses satellites to calculate an object's position

instrument panel A display of switches and dials for controlling other devices

law of physics A law of nature proven by science

log A record

mass The measure of how much matter something contains

mountain waves A strong movement of wind created by passing over mountains

navigation The planning, recording, controlling, and charting of a course for a ship or aircraft

nuclear reactor A container made for substances to mix and react together to create energy

pressure The force of something pressing on an object

procedure A series of steps for doing something

propeller A device with blades that is driven by an engine and powers an airplane

radar A device that uses the echo of radio waves to determine the location of an object

radiation Energy waves

radio room The main room in a ship where radio communications are held

rocket booster A solid fuel rocket attached to a main rocket to provide thrust

roll A maneuver in which an airplane rotates in the air

satellite A body that orbits the earth

simulator A device that mimics a real-life situation

static electricity An electric charge

taxi To go at a low speed along the ground or water

thermal A rising current of warm air

turbulence Stormy air caused by an air current moving against the flow of the main current

visibility The distance one can see in severe weather

wind shear A change in wind direction and speed between altitudes

World War I A war fought from 1914 to 1918 in Europe involving many countries

Index